COLLEGE LONDON PRESS

GRADE

GUITAR

Published by
Trinity College London Press Ltd
trinitycollege.com

Registered in England
Company no. 09726123

Photography by Zute Lightfoot, lightfootphoto.com

Printed in England by Caligraving Ltd

Parental and Teacher Guidance:

The songs in Trinity's Rock & Pop syllabus have been arranged
to represent the artists' original recordings as closely and
authentically as possible. Popular music frequently deals with
subject matter that some may find offensive or challenging.
It is possible that the songs may include material that some
might find unsuitable for use with younger learners.

We recommend that parents and teachers exercise their own
judgement to satisfy themselves that the lyrics of selected
songs are appropriate for the students concerned. As you
will be aware, there is no requirement that all songs in this
syllabus must be learned. Trinity does not associate itself with,
adopt or endorse any of the opinions or views expressed in
the selected songs.

THE EXAM AT A GLANCE

In your exam you will perform a set of three songs and one of the session skills assessments. You can choose the order of your set list.

SONG 1

Choose a song from this book.

SONG 2

Choose *either* a different song from this book
or a song from the list of additional Trinity Rock & Pop arrangements, available at trinityrock.com
or a song you have chosen yourself: this could be your own cover version or a song that you have written. It should be at the same level as the songs in this book and match the parameters at trinityrock.com

SONG 3: TECHNICAL FOCUS

Song 3 is designed to help you develop specific and relevant techniques in performance. Choose one of the technical focus songs from this book, which cover two specific technical elements.

SESSION SKILLS

Choose *either* **playback** *or* **improvising**.

Session skills are an essential part of every Rock & Pop exam. They are designed to help you develop the techniques music industry performers need.

Sample tests are available in our *Session Skills* books and free examples can be downloaded from trinityrock.com

ACCESS ALL AREAS

GET THE FULL ROCK & POP EXPERIENCE ONLINE AT TRINITYROCK.COM

We have created a range of digital resources to support your learning and give you insider information from the music industry, available online. You will find support, advice and digital content on:

- Songs, performance and technique
- Session skills
- The music industry

You can access tips and tricks from industry professionals featuring:

- Bite-sized videos that include tips from professional musicians on techniques used in the songs
- 'Producer's notes' on the tracks, to increase your knowledge of rock and pop
- Blog posts on performance tips, musical styles, developing technique and advice from the music industry

JOIN US ONLINE AT:

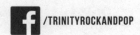 /TRINITYROCKANDPOP    @TRINITY_ROCK    /TRINITYROCKANDPOP   and at **TRINITYROCK.COM**

CONTENTS

THE AUDIO

Professional demo & backing tracks can be downloaded free, see inside cover for details.

Music preparation and book layout by Andrew Skirrow for Camden Music Services
Music consultants: Nick Crispin, Chris Walters, Christopher Hussey, Anders Rye
Drums recorded by Cab Grant and Jake Watson at AllStar Studios, Chelmsford
All other audio arranged, recorded & produced by Tom Fleming
Guitar arrangements by Tom Fleming

Musicians
Bass: Tom Fleming, Ben Heartland, Sam Burgess
Drums: George Double
Guitar: Tom Fleming
Vocals: Bo Walton, Alison Symons, Brendan Reilly

YOUR
PAGE
NOTES

COLD SWEAT
JAMES BROWN

WORDS AND MUSIC: JAMES BROWN, ALFRED 'PEE WEE' ELLIS

SINGLE BY
James Brown

ALBUM
Cold Sweat

B-SIDE
Cold Sweat - Part 2

RELEASED
July 1967

RECORDED
May 1967
King Studios, Cincinnati
Ohio, USA

LABEL
King

WRITERS
James Brown
Alfred 'Pee Wee' Ellis

PRODUCER
James Brown

The Godfather of Soul and the founder of funk, James Brown was born in South Carolina into a poor family. He started as a gospel singer in Georgia before joining a rhythm and blues group, and by the late '50s he had built a reputation as a dynamic frontman. One of the most important, innovative and prolific figures in music, he was a key influence for both Prince and Michael Jackson, not to mention hip-hop.

Recorded in May 1967 and released two months later, 'Cold Sweat' is often cited as the first true funk song, and its radical innovations changed the face of popular music. It was developed from an earlier Brown song called 'I Don't Care', from the 1962 album *Tour the USA*, the last of seven albums released under the name James Brown and the Famous Flames. In his 1986 autobiography, Brown said:

> It was a slow, bluesy tune then. It was good that way, but I was really getting into my funk bag now, and it became an almost completely different tune, except for the lyrics.

It was worked up by Brown with his bandleader, Pee Wee Ellis, who said:

> Between the two of us, we put it together one afternoon. He put the lyrics on it. The band set up in a semicircle in the studio with one microphone. It was recorded live in the studio. One take. It was like a performance. We didn't do overdubbing.

⚡ PERFORMANCE TIPS

A consistent rhythmic groove is a vital part of funk. Remember that you are part of the rhythm section, and here this means that you can make percussive sounds as well as melodic ones. This is partly notated for you in the muted notes, and you get a chance to create your own subtle variations from bar 23 onwards. Timing is everything with the hits in bars 29 and 31. The solo offers you a chance to ad lib — keep the groove strongly in mind as you do this.

COLD SWEAT

WORDS AND MUSIC:
JAMES BROWN, ALFRED 'PEE WEE' ELLIS

Intro

Funk ♩ = 110 (2 bars count-in)

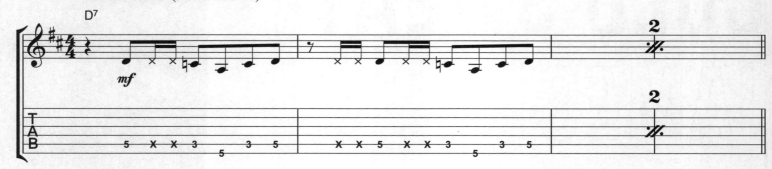

Verse

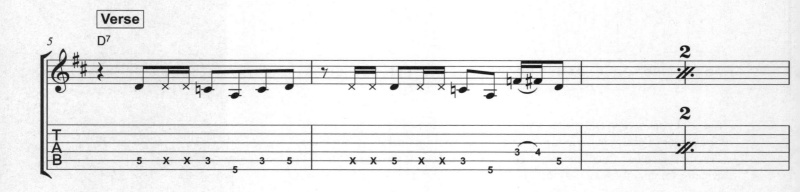

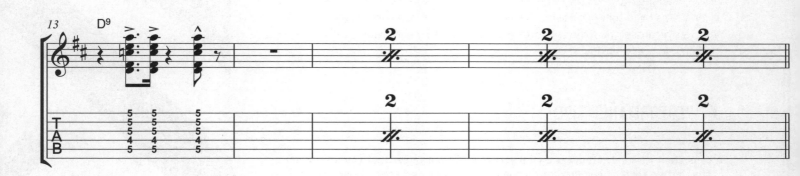

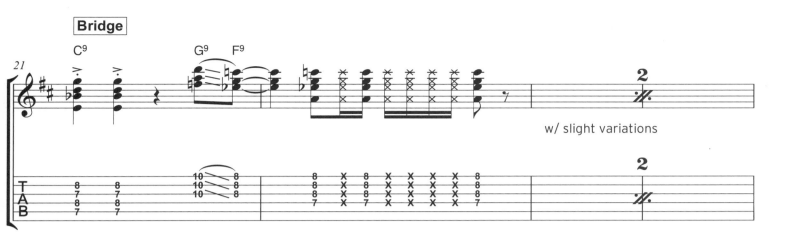

w/ slight variations

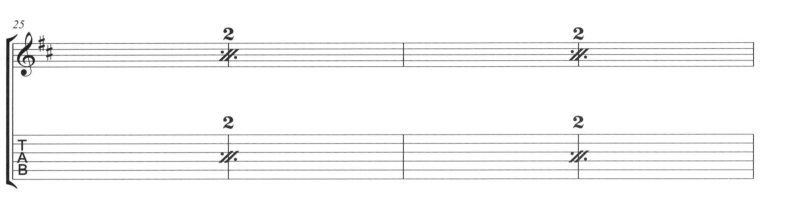

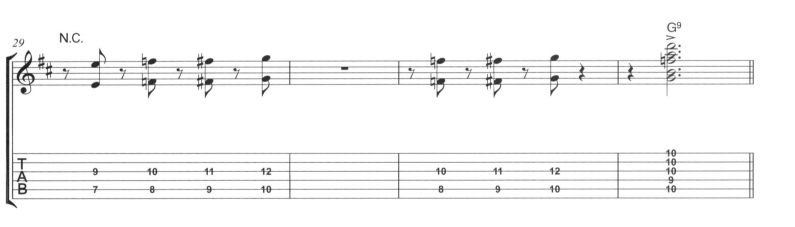

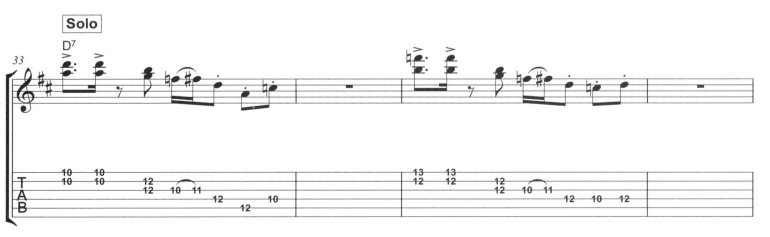

continue solo ad lib.

Bridge

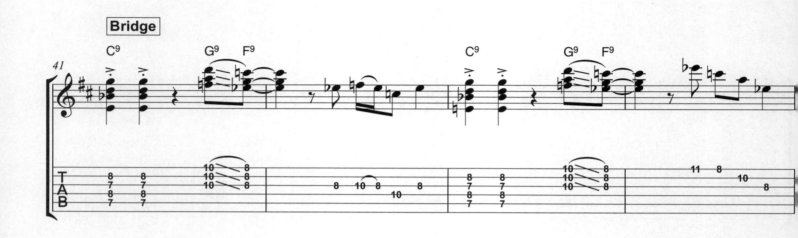

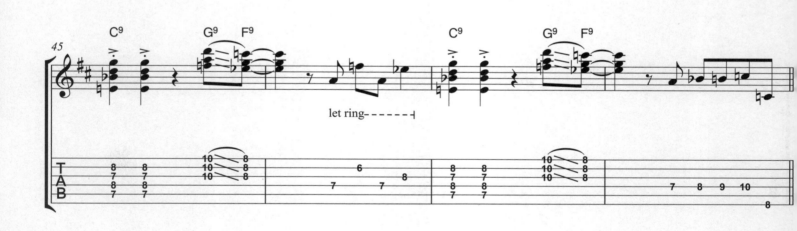

let ring- - - - - - -|

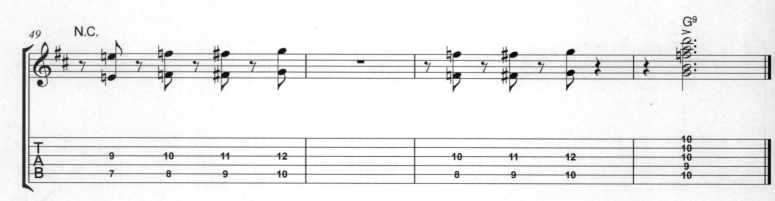

TECHNICAL FOCUS

DAY TRIPPER
THE BEATLES

WORDS AND MUSIC: JOHN LENNON, PAUL MCCARTNEY

SINGLE BY
The Beatles

B-SIDE
We Can Work It Out

RELEASED
3 December 1965

RECORDED
**16 October 1965
EMI Studios, London
England**

LABEL
Parlophone

WRITERS
**John Lennon
Paul McCartney**

PRODUCER
George Martin

Hailing from Liverpool, England, The Beatles released their first album, *Please Please Me*, in 1963, and by the mid '60s had become the world's biggest band. Acquiring the nickname the Fab Four along the way, the band comprised John Lennon, Paul McCartney, George Harrison and Ringo Starr. Their impact, success, achievements and influence dominates popular music to this day.

A collaborative effort between Lennon and McCartney based on Lennon's idea, 'Day Tripper' was recorded on 16 October 1965 and released on 3 December that year, together with 'We Can Work It Out' as the first ever double A-side single. Released on the same day as the group's sixth album, *Rubber Soul*, neither song featured on that album. This practice followed 1963's 'From Me to You', 'She Loves You' and 'I Want to Hold Your Hand' and 1964's 'I Feel Fine', all of which were released as standalone singles in the UK. The two songs were counted separately on the US Billboard chart, where 'We Can Work It Out' became the band's 11th No. 1 and 'Day Tripper' peaked at No. 5.

TECHNICAL FOCUS

Two technical focus elements are featured in this song:

- Riff playing
- Bends

This song has a classic riff which will test your **riff playing**. Not only does the riff have to be stylish and consistent in order to set up the groove, but you also have to maintain these qualities as the riff travels through different harmonies and positions. The solo offers different tests of your **bends**, featuring both individual bends and a held bend.

TECHNICAL FOCUS
DAY TRIPPER

WORDS AND MUSIC:
JOHN LENNON, PAUL MCCARTNEY

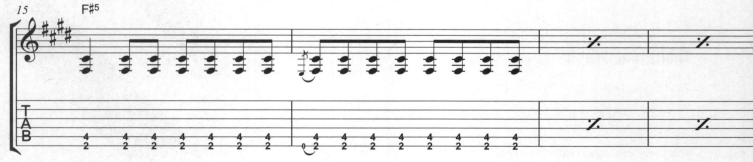

Coda

Outro Chorus

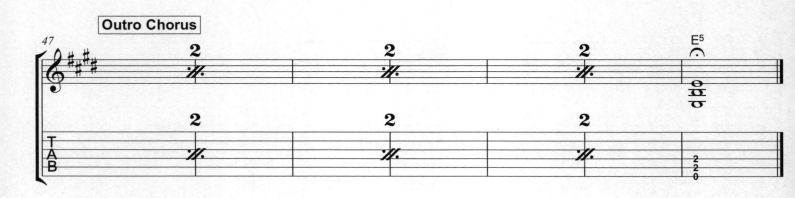

DESIRE

U2

WORDS: BONO. MUSIC: U2

04 GRADE
GUITAR

SINGLE BY
U2

ALBUM
Rattle and Hum

B-SIDE
Hallelujah (Here She Comes)

RELEASED
26 September 1988

RECORDED
**1987-1988
STS Studios, Dublin
Ireland (album)**

LABEL
Island

WRITERS
**U2 (music)
Bono (lyrics)**

PRODUCER
Jimmy Lovine

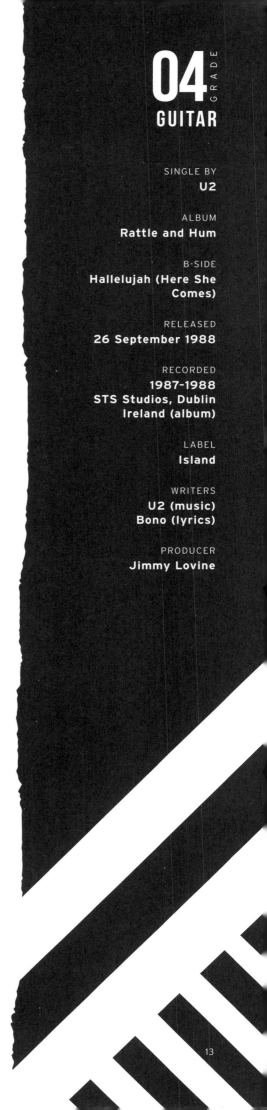

Hailing from Dublin, Ireland, U2 are among the top ten best-selling bands in the history of popular music. Their line-up has remained unchanged since the release of their debut EP in 1979, comprising singer Bono, guitarist The Edge, bassist Adam Clayton and drummer Larry Mullen Jr.

Released as the lead single from U2's sixth album, 1988's *Rattle and Hum*, 'Desire' became the band's first No. 1 hit in both the UK and Australia, something they had already achieved twice the previous year in America with 'With or Without You' and 'I Still Haven't Found What I'm Looking For'. Based upon the 'Bo Diddley beat', a distinctive rhythm featured on everything from The Rolling Stones' 'Not Fade Away' to George Michael's 'Faith', The Edge took inspiration for the riff from The Stooges' '1969'. Speaking in 1988, the guitarist said:

> What I like about 'Desire' is that if there's ever been a cool No. 1 to have in the UK, that's it, because it's totally not what people are listening to or what's in the charts at the moment. It's a rock'n'roll record – in no way is it a pop song.

It won the band a Grammy and helped secure their second No. 1 album in both the UK and US.

⚡ PERFORMANCE TIPS

The intro of this song has a number of challenges – timing, accuracy and muted chords. Aim to achieve a natural, relaxed feel once you have mastered the complexity of these elements. Later there is a short solo to look out for – play this with projection to bring out the sound of the double-stopping.

DESIRE

WORDS: BONO. **MUSIC:** U2

Intro

Rock ♩ = 110 (2 bars count-in)

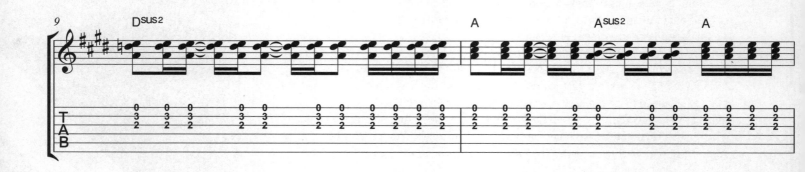

Verse

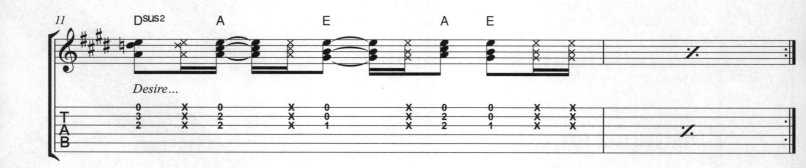

Desire…

Breakdown

Chorus

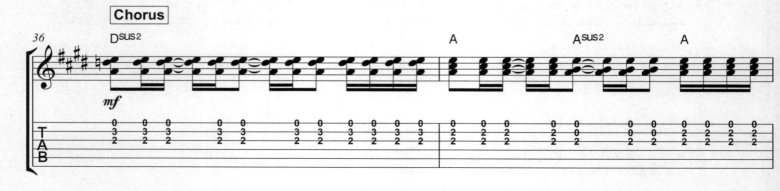

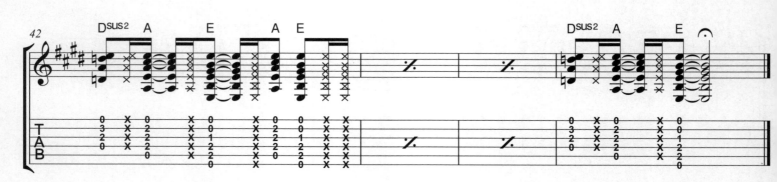

HOLD ON
ALABAMA SHAKES

WORDS AND MUSIC: BRITTANY HOWARD

SINGLE BY
Alabama Shakes

ALBUM
Boys & Girls

RELEASED
6 February 2012

RECORDED
2011
The Bomb Shelter
Nashville, Tennessee
USA

LABEL
ATO (USA)
Rough Trade (UK)

WRITER
Brittany Howard

PRODUCERS
Andrija Tokic
Alabama Shakes

Alabama Shakes are a blues-rock quartet from Athens, Alabama. Led by powerhouse vocalist and guitarist Brittany Howard, the band also includes Heath Fogg on guitar, Zac Cockrell on bass and Steve Johnson on drums. 'Hold On' was the band's first single, and the opening song on their 2012 debut album *Boys & Girls*. The album reached No. 3 in the UK and No. 6 in the US, earning the band three Grammy nominations and the main support slot on a number of US tour dates with one of their heroes, Jack White.

With a gritty mix of soul, blues and rock, Alabama Shakes' exhilarating live performances and Howard's stand-out star quality helped ensure the band's swift ascent. *Rolling Stone* named 'Hold On' as No. 1 in its '50 best songs of 2012' list, likening Howard's singing to 'a husky moaning-in-the-moonlight drawl'.

⚡ PERFORMANCE TIPS

You'll need to settle quickly into this song's laid-back groove, an important part of establishing its blues-rock feel. The chorus features a more complex semiquaver riff, which uses hammer-ons to give an accented, cross-rhythm feel. Look out for the held bend in bar 19, which will help you to create an authentic bluesy sound. The outro chords will require precision.

HOLD ON

WORDS AND MUSIC: BRITTANY HOWARD

Outro

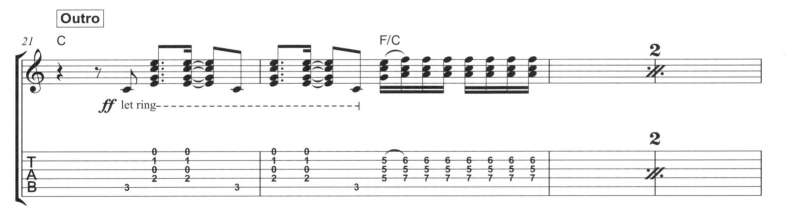

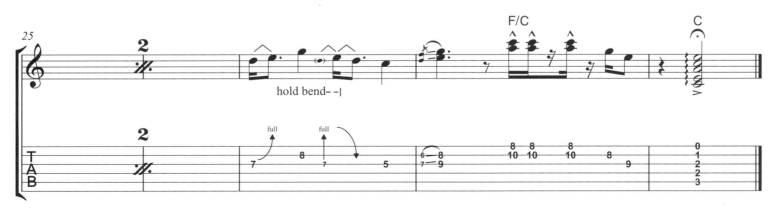

SINGLE BY
The Cult

ALBUM
Love

B-SIDE
**No. 13
She Sells Sanctuary
(Long Version)
The Snake
She Sells Sanctuary
(Howling Mix)
Assault On Sanctuary**

RELEASED
17 May 1985

LABEL
Beggars Banquet

WRITERS
**Ian Astbury
Billy Duffy**

PRODUCER
Steve Brown

TECHNICAL FOCUS

SHE SELLS SANCTUARY

THE CULT

WORDS AND MUSIC: IAN ASTBURY, WILLIAM DUFFY

Following the demise of his early-80s band Southern Death Cult, singer Ian Astbury joined forces with guitarist Billy Duffy to form Death Cult before finalising their name as The Cult in 1984. Inspired by Led Zeppelin and The Doors, their finely honed hard rock sound has yielded a successful career, still going strong after more than 30 years.

'She Sells Sanctuary' was released in May 1985 and climbed to No. 15 in the UK within three months. It was the first single to be released from their top-five hit album *Love* and the last song to be recorded with drummer Nigel Preston who was replaced by Mark Brzezicki of Big Country. Its distinctive sound came about after Duffy found a violin bow in the studio, he comments:

> I started to play the guitar with the bow like Jimmy Page. I just hit every pedal I had on the pedal board. Then once I stopped banging the strings I played the middle section of the song, which was kind of a pick thing with all the BOSS pedals on, and that sound just leaped out. The producer went, 'Hold it, that's great!' And we decided to start the song with that mystical sound. If I hadn't found that violin bow lying around, we wouldn't have gone there.

TECHNICAL FOCUS

Two technical focus elements are featured in this song:

- String crossing
- cross-beat accents

This song features an iconic riff for the guitar, which includes lots of **position shifts** up and down the neck. Watch for accuracy at the start as you cross between the open D string and the other fretted notes and think about which fingers to use as you change position. Be sure to feel the placement of the **cross-beat accents** at the verse with precision. Note also the use of palm muting here to emphasise the difference between the accented and non-accented notes.

TECHNICAL FOCUS

SHE SELLS SANCTUARY

WORDS AND MUSIC:
IAN ASTBURY, WILLIAM DUFFY

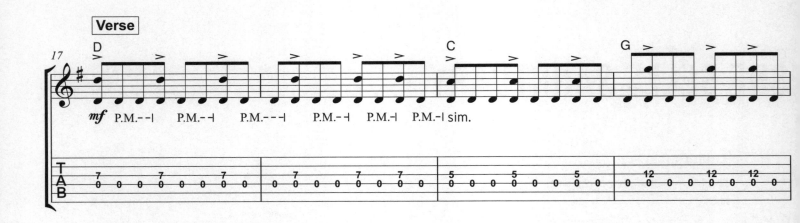

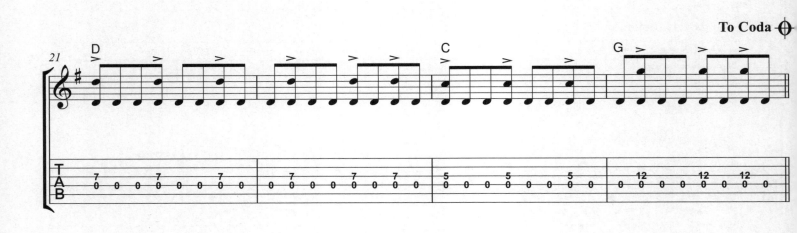

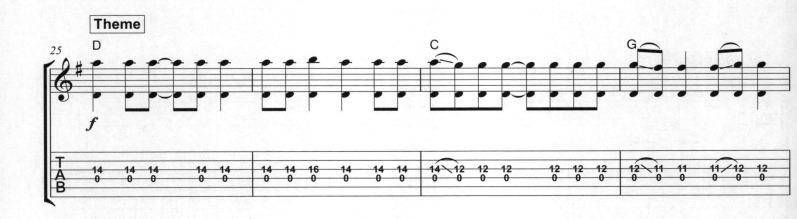

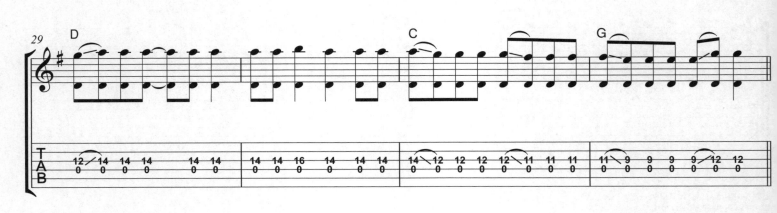

Verse/Chorus

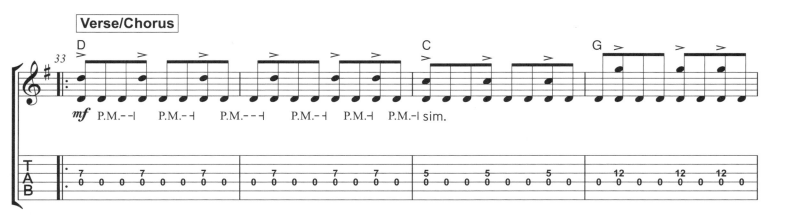

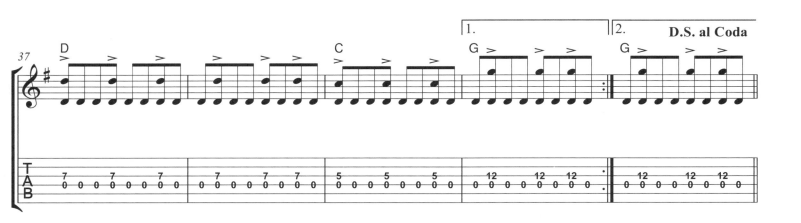

Coda

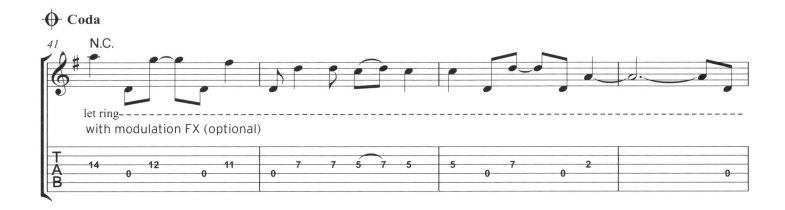

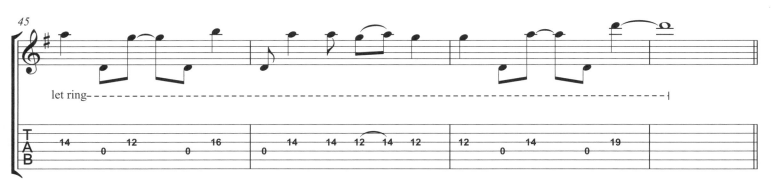

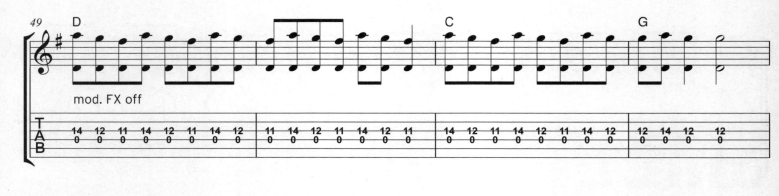

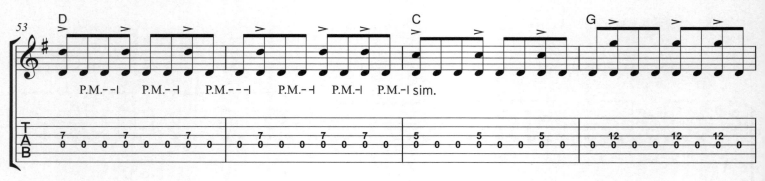

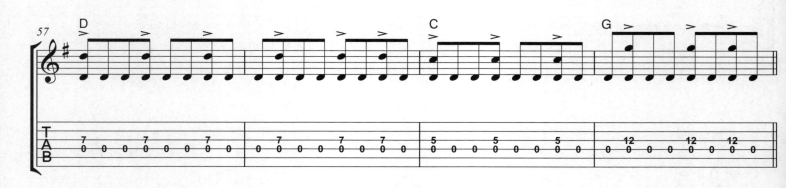

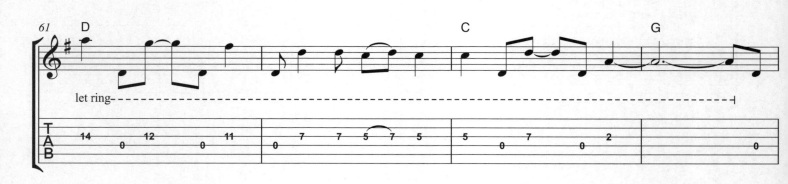

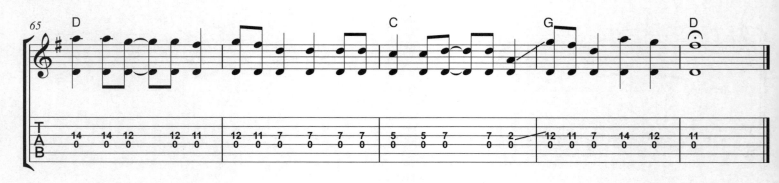

SMELLS LIKE TEEN SPIRIT
NIRVANA

WORDS AND MUSIC: KURT COBAIN, KRIST NOVOSELIC DAVE GROHL

SINGLE BY
Nirvana

ALBUM
Nevermind

B-SIDE
**Drain You
Even in His Youth
Aneurysm**

RELEASED
10 September 1991

RECORDED
**May 1991, Sound City
Studios, Van Nuys
California, USA**

LABEL
DGC Records

WRITERS
**Kurt Cobain
Krist Novoselic
Dave Grohl**

PRODUCER
Butch Vi

Please note: This song contains subject matter that some might find inappropriate for younger learners. Please refer to the Parental and Teacher Guidance at the beginning of this book for more information.

Powerhouse rock trio Nirvana exploded out of the burgeoning Seattle grunge scene of the late 80s with the release of their second album, 1991's *Nevermind*. The band were fronted by the intense figure of Kurt Cobain, whose songwriting gift and expressive voice turned the initially cult band into overnight sensations, and saw a reluctant Cobain cast as spokesman for a generation.

Released two weeks ahead of *Nevermind*, 'Smells Like Teen Spirit' was not just a global top-ten hit but a cultural phenomenon. In an interview with *Rolling Stone*, published three months before his death, Cobain said of the song:

> I was trying to write the ultimate pop song. I was basically trying to rip off the Pixies. I have to admit it... We used their sense of dynamics, being soft and quiet and then loud and hard.

The famous 'Here we are now, entertain us' line came from something Cobain 'used to say every time I used to walk into a party to break the ice.' Kathleen Hanna, the lead singer of the group Bikini Kill, gave Cobain the idea for the title when she wrote 'Kurt Smells Like Teen Spirit' on his bedroom wall. Cobain was unaware that Teen Spirit was in fact a brand of deodorant.

⚡ PERFORMANCE TIPS

This song is all about balancing a wild quality with accuracy. Think about playing in a way that is rough but not messy – it's a challenging balance to strike! Pay attention to the muted notes at the start, which are important in creating the rhythmic feel. At bar 9 the character changes with a lonely-sounding guitar idea. Later, look out for the fourth-string bends in the solo passage.

25

SMELLS LIKE TEEN SPIRIT

WORDS AND MUSIC: KURT COBAIN
KRIST NOVOSELIC, DAVE GROHL

TECHNICAL FOCUS

ROCKIN' IN THE FREE WORLD

NEIL YOUNG

WORDS AND MUSIC: NEIL YOUNG

SINGLE BY
Neil Young

ALBUM
Freedom

B-SIDE
**Rockin' in the Free World
(live acoustic)**

RELEASED
**2 October 1989 (album)
14 November 1989 (single)**

RECORDED
25 July 1988 - 10 July 1989

**Redwood Digital, Broken
Arrow Ranch, Woodside
California, USA**

**The Hit Factory, New York
City, New York, USA
(album)**

LABEL
Reprise

WRITER
Neil Young

PRODUCERS
**Neil Young
Niko Bolas**

Neil Young is a Canadian musician and internationally successful solo artist from Toronto whose recording career spans six decades. One of the most distinctive voices and guitarists in rock, he first gained recognition for his involvement with the band Buffalo Springfield in the mid-60s and then as one quarter of Crosby, Stills, Nash and Young.

'Rockin' in the Free World' was both the first and last song on his 1989 album *Freedom*, the first a solo acoustic version performed live in concert, the second an electric studio version recorded with a band. Acoustic/electric bookends of the same song were something Young had introduced on 1979's *Rust Never Sleeps* album. The title was inspired by a comment from Frank 'Poncho' Sampedro, guitarist with his regular backing band Crazy Horse, who was later given a songwriting credit for providing the title. Young performed 'Rockin' in the Free World' at London's Wembley Stadium as part of the Nelson Mandela tribute concert on 16 April 1990, two months after the South African leader's release from prison after 27 years of captivity.

TECHNICAL FOCUS

Two technical focus elements are featured in this song:

- Clean picking
- Unison bend

Clean picking is needed in the verse of this song, which combines arpeggio figures with chords. You'll need to avoid striking unwanted strings, and aim to create an even sound where the single notes are not too quiet compared to the chords. The solo features **unison bends**, held for one bar of repeated quavers. These need to be rhythmically accurate, with both notes of the unison clearly audible.

TECHNICAL FOCUS
ROCKIN' IN THE FREE WORLD

WORDS AND MUSIC: NEIL YOUNG

YOUR
PAGE
NOTES

YOU KNOW I'M NO GOOD AMY WINEHOUSE

WORDS AND MUSIC: AMY WINEHOUSE

SINGLE BY
Amy Winehouse

ALBUM
Back to Black

B-SIDE
**To Know Him is to
Love Him (live)
Monkey Man
You Know I'm No Good
(Skeewiff Mix)**

RELEASED
**27 October 2006 (album)
5 January 2007 (single)**

RECORDED
**2005-2006
Chung King Studio
New York City
New York, USA
Daptone Studios
Brooklyn, New York, USA
Metropolis Studios
London, England**

LABEL
Island

WRITER
Amy Winehouse

PRODUCER
Mark Ronson

One of the most distinctive and successful singer-songwriters of her generation, Amy Winehouse was born in London, England in 1983. She followed her 2003 debut album *Frank* with 2006's hugely successful and Grammy Award-winning *Back to Black*, a critical and commercial hit that launched her to international stardom but would prove to be her final release.

One of the highlights of Winehouse's *Back to Black*, 'You Know I'm No Good' was released as the second single from the Mark Ronson-produced album after the instant classic 'Rehab'. Both recordings featured many members of Brooklyn funk/soul band The Dap-Kings, including drummer Homer Steinweiss, keyboard player Victor Axelrod, guitarists Binky Griptite and Thomas Brenneck and bandleader/arranger Gabriel Roth. Dap-Kings members also provided the notable brass parts. The album topped the UK album chart on four occasions, becoming the UK's best-selling album of 2007 and returning to the top, one final time, for three weeks following Winehouse's tragic death in July 2011. It remains the second best-selling album of the 21st century in the UK, only Adele's *21* having outsold it.

⚡ PERFORMANCE TIPS

This song has a number of technical challenges to keep you busy. At the start, play the quavers evenly and accurately, counting the syncopations carefully in bars 17 and 19. Later there are lots of slides, first on three-note chords and then on parallel octaves. These will need to be played with accuracy and confidence.

YOU KNOW I'M NO GOOD

WORDS AND MUSIC: AMY WINEHOUSE

CHOOSING SONGS FOR YOUR EXAM

SONG 1

Choose a song from this book.

SONG 2

Choose a song which is:

Either a different song from this book

or from the list of additional Trinity Rock & Pop arrangements, available at trinityrock.com

or from a printed or online source

or your own arrangement

or a song that you have written yourself

You can play Song 2 unaccompanied or with a backing track (minus the guitar part). If you like, you can create a backing track yourself (or with friends), add your own vocals, or be accompanied live by another musician.

The level of difficulty and length of the song should be similar to the songs in this book and match the parameters available at trinityrock.com

When choosing a song, think about:

* Does it work on my instrument?

* Are there any technical elements that are too difficult for me? (If so, perhaps save it for when you do the next grade)

* Do I enjoy playing it?

* Does it work with my other songs to create a good set list?

SONG 3: TECHNICAL FOCUS

Song 3 is designed to help you develop specific and relevant techniques in performance. Choose one of the technical focus songs from this book, which cover two specific technical elements.

SHEET MUSIC

If your choice for Song 2 is not from this book, you must provide the examiner with a photocopy. The title, writers of the song and your name should be on the sheet music. You must also bring an original copy of the book, or a download version with proof of purchase, for each song that you perform in the exam.

Your music can be:

* A lead sheet with lyrics, chords and melody line

* A chord chart with lyrics

* A full score using conventional staff notation

PLAYING WITH BACKING TRACKS

All your backing tracks can be downloaded from soundwise.co.uk

- The backing tracks begin with a click track, which sets the tempo and helps you start accurately

- Be careful to balance the volume of the backing track against your instrument

- Listen carefully to the backing track to ensure that you are playing in time

If you are creating your own backing track, here are some further tips:

- Make sure that the sound quality is of a good standard

- Think carefully about the instruments/sounds you are using on the backing track

- Avoid copying what you are playing in the exam on the backing track – it should support, not duplicate

- Do you need to include a click track at the beginning?

COPYRIGHT IN A SONG

If you are a singer, instrumentalist or songwriter it is important to know about copyright. When someone writes a song they automatically own the copyright (sometimes called 'the rights'). Copyright begins once a piece of music has been documented or recorded (eg by video, CD or score notation) and protects the interests of the creators. This means that others cannot copy it, sell it, make it available online or record it without the owner's permission or the appropriate licence.

COVER VERSIONS

- When an artist creates a new version of a song it is called a 'cover version'

- The majority of songwriters subscribe to licensing agencies, also known as 'collecting societies'. When a songwriter is a member of such an agency, the performing rights to their material are transferred to the agency (this includes cover versions of their songs)

- The agency works on the writer's behalf by issuing licences to performance venues, who report what songs have been played, which in turn means that the songwriter will receive a payment for any songs used

- You can create a cover version of a song and use it in an exam without needing a licence

There are different rules for broadcasting (eg TV, radio, internet), selling or copying (pressing CDs, DVDs etc), and for printed material, and the appropriate licences should be sought out.

YOUR
PAGE
NOTES

YOUR
PAGE
NOTES